Philip Meadows Taylor

A memoir of the family of Taylor of Norwich

Philip Meadows Taylor

A memoir of the family of Taylor of Norwich

ISBN/EAN: 9783337723903

Printed in Europe, USA, Canada, Australia, Japan

Cover: Foto ©ninafisch / pixelio.de

More available books at **www.hansebooks.com**

A MEMOIR

OF THE

FAMILY OF TAYLOR

OF NORWICH

BY

PHILIP MEADOWS TAYLOR

OF LE MAS D'AZIL

PRIVATELY PRINTED

1886

PREFACE.

The following Memoirs of the past generation of the Taylor family of Norwich form a part of a larger work relating to my own life.

This will explain why my own personality takes a rather too prominent position in this record of our forefathers, which has been printed apart for the members of the family.

P. M. T.

Le Mas d'Azil:
August 20, 1886.

A MEMOIR

OF THE

TAYLOR FAMILY OF NORWICH.

———◦✦◦———

My name is Philip Meadows Taylor; I was born in the second decade of the century; I belong to that old Presbyterian and Whig family, the Taylors of Norwich.

I will only glance at a family legend of our ancestors coming to England with William the Conqueror. Quillebœuf is near a dangerous part of the river Seine, where the shifting sands caused boats to be delayed or wrecked, within reach of the castle of Robert le Diable, and from this town our legendary progenitor came. Be that as it may, our family were living in Lancashire in the seventeenth century, and it was in that county, in the year 1694, that Dr. John Taylor, my historical ancestor, was born.

He was well known as a nonconformist divine, as the author of the Hebrew Concordance and a treatise on the Epistle of St. Paul to the Romans, as well as of other theological works.

His son Richard married Margaret, daughter and coheiress of Mr. Philip Meadows, who was Mayor of Norwich in 1734. This gentleman, though a staunch Presbyterian, was a somewhat lax nonconformist; a statute of George I. passed in 1718 allowed dissenters to aspire to municipal honours, and in 1724 we find him Sheriff of Norwich. He was a man of good natural parts, a useful member of society, and an accomplished mathematician, spending much thought on the vexed problem of the longitude.

Mr. Philip Meadows embarked a large part of his fortune in the South Sea scheme, of course only to lose it; and his son-in-law, Richard Taylor, who was in the wool trade, lost the greater part of his fortune in the great earthquake of Lisbon in 1755.

Philip Meadows was a son of John Meadows of Ousdon, a nonconformist minister who was ejected in 1662.

A younger brother of the ejected minister was so remarkable a man that I must give a short sketch of his career. Sir Philip Meadows was a younger son with little or no fortune, but nature had endowed him with great intellectual gifts and great tenacity of purpose, and he received a good education.　Through the patronage of Thurloe he was appointed joint Latin secretary to the Council of State under the Commonwealth, with *John Milton*, and in 1655 I find him translating the Swedish Treaty negotiated by Whitelock.　In 1657 he was sent on a delicate mission of pacification between Denmark and Sweden, and Sweden and Poland, and he brought to a conclusion the Treaty of Oliva; subsequently he had to conduct negotiations at some of the German courts.　Frederic III. of Denmark gave him the order of Knighthood of the Elephant as a signal mark of favour.

Sir Philip Meadows served under the brief protectorate of Richard Cromwell, and later on was so acceptable to Charles II. that he was appointed Knight Marshal and Comptroller of the Army Accounts.　These important posts he held under Charles II., James II., William and Mary, and Queen Anne, dying at the age of ninety-three in 1718.　The Meadows family were a long-lived race.

The son and grandson bore the same title and held the same posts.　His great-nephew, Admiral Charles Meadows, took his mother's name of Pierre-

pont, and was raised to the peerage by the title of
Baron Pierrepont and Viscount Newark in 1796,
and advanced to the dignity of Earl Manvers in
1806.

I now return to Richard Taylor, who married
Margaret Meadows. This lady's mother was Margaret, daughter of John Hall of Norwich and Margaret Lombe, cousin to Sir Thomas Lombe, Sheriff
of London in 1728. His name, with that of his
brother John Lombe, is noteworthy in connection
with the introduction of silk manufactures into
England.

In those days the laws of Piedmont inflicted the
penalty of death on any person who should attempt
to carry out of the kingdom drawings or models of
the *organsin*, or silk-twisting machinery, which was
a special industry in Piedmont. John Lombe
mastered the rough dialect of the country, assumed
the dress of a peasant, and obtained employment in
the silk mills. Cautiously and slowly during the
night watches he cut tiny paper models of each
part of the machinery protected by such stern
enactments. These precious bits of paper were
placed in his snuff-box and hidden under a layer of
tobacco; this was in 1718. I well remember, some
sixty years ago, being taken by my father to the

Tower of London and shown the two first *organsin* mills built by John Lombe after his return. Are they still in existence?

Curiously enough, in the years 1830-40 my father took an active part in introducing new machinery for silk in Piedmont, making known the system of treating the cocoons by steam.

To return to John Meadows. He was three times married; his second wife, the mother of his children, was Sarah Fairfax — the Lord-General Fairfax of Parliamentary renown was of the same stock. To Sarah Fairfax we are indebted for a series of admirable reflections on the education of her children.

The Fairfaxes are an old Yorkshire family, of which a younger branch settled in Norfolk and Suffolk. In 1662 Benjamin and his sons, John and Nathaniel Fairfax, were among the ejected nonconformist ministers, for the Fairfaxes—like the Lombes, the Meadowses, and the Taylors—were Presbyterians in religion and Whigs in politics. I pride myself on being descended from such a stock.

Another daughter of Philip Meadows, Sarah, married Mr. David Martineau, grandson of Gaston Martineau, who fled from France at the time of the revocation of the Edict of Nantes. Mrs. Richard

Taylor and Mrs. David Martineau had eight children each ; they were left widows at an early age ; they lived near one another, devoting their lives to the careful training of their children, for which they were well fitted by their strong intelligence and high culture. I find record of five sons of Sarah Martineau ; of these the eldest, Philip Meadows, was a celebrated surgeon, known to be a very skilful operator. Thomas, the youngest, is remarkable as the father of Dr. James Martineau, the distinguished writer and preacher, and of Harriet Martineau, whose works are popular in the United States as well as in the old country. David and Peter were sugar-refiners in London. John, the fourth son, was an eminent brewer, and became a partner in the house of Whitbread & Co.

A brother of these two ladies, another Philip Meadows, was a much-respected lawyer at Diss ; he left no children, but was succeeded in his practice by a nephew, Mr. Meadows Taylor, fourth son of Mr. and Mrs. Richard Taylor. Mr. Meadows Taylor and his uncle carried on their practice for a period of ninety-eight years, from 1740 to 1838, when Mr. Meadows Taylor died esteemed and respected by all who knew him.

Mr. Meadows Taylor married Miss Dyson, a

member of a much-respected Norfolk family; their
son, Thomas Lombe Taylor, presented to his native
town a very handsome building, called the Corn
Hall, but with assembly-rooms and library forming
part of the building. One of his sons, Francis, who
married his cousin Susan, daughter of Dr. Rigby,
is now (1886) member for South Norfolk. He is
well known to yachtsmen as the owner of the
' Tara.'

Mr. John Rigby of Lancaster married Sarah,
daughter of Dr. John Taylor; their daughter
married Dr. Caleb Hillier Parry, a physician of
celebrity at Bath, and was mother of the great
Arctic explorer, Sir William Edward Parry, born
1790, died at Ems, 1855.

An anecdote preserved in the Dyson family is
deserving of record. About 1755 the Marquis de
Lafayette, father of the celebrated general, applied
to his English friends to obtain for him the services
of a competent tutor to teach his son agriculture
as practised in England. Mr. John Dyson was the
person chosen, and he lived for some years with
the Lafayette family on the most agreeable footing.
But no peaceful career was that of his pupil, and in
1792 the young revolutionary General Lafayette,
after playing a conspicuous part in the American

and French revolutions, was captured by the Aus-
trians and imprisoned in the fortress of Olmütz.
His devoted wife used all possible means to obtain
his release, and at last bethought her of help from
General Washington. There was the greatest difficulty in communicating with the United States,
and she appealed to Mr. John Dyson to assist
her. He succeeded in sending her two letters to the
President. General Washington replied to the first
letter only; copies of these two touching appeals
are in the possession of the Dyson family.

I must allow myself to mention that my wife is
a goddaughter of General Lafayette, and that part
of my honeymoon was spent in his family.

We will now return to Mr. and Mrs. Richard Taylor's eight children. Philip, the eldest, was, with his
cousin Rigby, put to a school at Nantwich under the
care of Mr. Priestly, afterwards celebrated as author
and chemist, and known as Dr. Priestly. Philip became a Presbyterian minister, and in 1774 was appointed minister of the Eustacè Street congregation,
and settled at Harold's Cross, near Dublin; he
married Miss Weld, and died in 1831, greatly loved
and respected. He was the grandfather of Colonel
Philip Meadows Taylor, the author of ' Confessions
of a Thug,' ' Tara,' &c. His Autobiography narrates

the events of a very remarkable life, but it does not contain the following anecdote. Colonel Taylor was engaged to a daughter of Mr. Palmer, head of the great banking-house of Calcutta and Hyderabad. When everything was settled for the marriage, a sudden and tremendous change came over the fortunes of the firm, and Mr. Palmer told Colonel Taylor he had his full permission to relinquish the marriage now that his daughter was portionless. My true-hearted cousin refused to sacrifice his love, and the marriage took place. Colonel Taylor was selected to administer the Shorapoor State during the minority of the Rajah, from 1843 to 1853. In 1869 Her Majesty was pleased to appoint Colonel Taylor Companion of the Star of India. His health, sorely tried by Indian work and climate, gave way, and he died in 1876.

John, the second son of Richard Taylor, born in 1750, was my grandfather. He married in 1777 Susannah, daughter of Mr. John Cook of Norwich. Mr. John Taylor was strongly attached to the faith of his forefathers, and he was a staunch supporter of the Whig party; but although in those days party feeling ran high and religious prejudices were strong, he was of so kind and genial a temper, that eminent persons of different opinions came with

pleasure to his house—Sir James MacIntosh, Sir
James Smith, Mr. Crabbe Robinson, Dr. Southey
(brother of the laureate), Mr. Windham, Sir Thomas
Beevor, Mrs. Fry, and the Gurney family, Mrs.
Opie, Mrs. Barbauld (who wrote those touching
lines on the death of Mrs. Martineau), and other
Norwich worthies.

My grandmother united strength of will and
great acquirements to a kindly nature and a loving
heart, and she contributed to making her husband's
house a favourite gathering-place for his numerous
friends. My grandfather was no contemptible poet ;
some of his hymns are beautiful.

> Exulting, rejoicing, hail the happy morning,
> The morn of the day when our Christ was born,

adapted to the air of 'Adeste Fideles,' ought to
take its place in every hymn-book.

He was no less happy in his political songs—

> The trumpet of liberty sounds through the world,
> And the Universe starts at the sound.

He is said to have written this spirit-stirring lyric
on the back of a letter which announced the fall of
the Bastile, July 1789. For my part, I prefer it to
Rouget de l'Isle's lines,

> Qu'un sang impur arrose vos sillons ;

but those who have heard the Marseillaise sung amidst the gloom and turmoil of revolutionary war may well deem its words hateful.

The 'Trumpet of Liberty' was not, however, acceptable to the Tory ministers of the day, as its author knew, though it was first sung by him at a dinner presided over by a royal Duke. At another dinner, also presided over by that liberal and independent prince the Duke of Sussex, with Lord Albemarle, Sir Francis Burdett, and Mr. Coke of Holkham among the guests, the Duke called on Mr. Taylor for the 'Trumpet of Liberty.' 'No, please your Royal Highness,' answered my grandfather, 'you know I got into trouble before.' 'Never fear,' said the burly prince, 'my back is broad enough to protect you.'

The Taylor and Martineau families were at the head of the Whig party in Norwich, and the county magnates, the Earl of Albemarle and the Squire of Holkham, large-hearted men, gave their help in returning Whig members for the borough. Mr. William Smith sat for Norwich, I believe, forty years, and this of course before the Reform Bill, though as early as 1822 reform had many stout adherents in Norfolk.

I love to dwell on my childish days passed

under my grandfather's roof, and still remember some of the stories told of his friends and acquaintances.

It appeared that county members had in those days the right to present themselves at levées and drawing-rooms in top-boots and breeches. This privilege Mr. Coke declined to forego, much to the disgust of that fine gentleman, the Prince Regent.

Of one of the great bankers at Norwich they told this story: He was at my grandfather's, playing a quiet rubber, when an officious clerk rushed in and whispered that the London mail had just brought the news of the failure of a large banking establishment by which his firm would sustain a considerable loss. The great banker took no notice, but went on with his whist. When the game had ended, he turned round to the clerk, and said, 'What did you mean by interrupting me? You have made me lose *the trick*.' The stakes were two pence, be it known, and of course it was long whist.

Then there was the adventure of the apron. A learned divine, very absent and rather short-sighted, found himself at a dinner-table seated next to a young lady, or rather a lady who had been young, and who kept up the fashion of

embroidered muslin aprons. The divine's dress
was also that of the period, a period when napkins
had not come into use. After doing justice to the
good things on the table, his eyes were attracted by
something wrong—some strange patch of white,
where all should have been black. He muttered,
' Been careless in dressing, dear, dear ! ' then he
began to impound the waif or stray, rather astonished
at the amount of tugging it required. Meanwhile the lady became more and more uneasy, till
the brilliant idea of unhooking her apron occurred.
The doctor pocketed the whole, and only wondered,
when he divested himself of his black knee-breeches
at night, how that mysterious muslin got there.

In 1784 my grandfather, in concert with his
cousin, Mr. P. M. Martineau, gave active support
in establishing that excellent institution, the Norwich
Public Library.

Though a very abstemious man, my grandfather
was in his later years a sufferer from severe fits of
gout, and it was somewhat of an effort when in
June, 1826, he determined to pay my father a visit
at Corngreaves in Staffordshire. Father and son
met at Birmingham on a Sunday morn—well do I
remember the fatal day. They attended divine
service, and then started in my father's car, which

opened behind. At the steep descent of Halesowen,
'York,' the horse, became unmanageable. Turner,
the coachman, was thrown from the box; my father,
in attempting to reach the box and recover the
reins, was jerked out, falling on his head; and my
grandfather in attempting to get out behind caught
his foot in the step, and fell heavily on the ground.
When my father recovered his senses and went to
his assistance, he was insensible. He was lifted up
and carried to the house of a kind old Quaker hard
by, and never left that house alive. Well do I
remember standing with my mother and sister at
the gate waiting the arrival of the travellers, but the
carriage which drove down the hill at headlong speed
was not theirs; it was that of the good old Quaker,
Mr. Brewen. He gently led my mother inside, and
then they reappeared and drove off to Halesowen,
where he installed my mother; and telling his
daughter and his niece to pack up clothes for a
short absence, had the horses put to his carriage,
and left the house, writing a short note to explain
that as rooms would be required for the doctor and
the relations, he had thought it desirable to advance
by a few days an intended journey, and he placed
his house entirely at the disposal of the Taylor
family. My grandfather breathed his last on the

23rd June, his sons standing around him, and I, a lad, among them. It was my first experience of death. How many dear ones have I watched breathe their last since!

I should mention that the death of my grand-mother took place in 1823.

The eldest son, born in 1779, was called John after his father. His mother encouraged his boyish taste for mechanical pursuits by giving him mathe-matical instruments and a turning lathe, thus de-termining his career. At the early age of nineteen, after a training as land surveyor, friends who were shareholders in the ' Wheal Friendship ' mine near Tavistock, struck by his intelligence, judgment, and integrity, placed that important concern under his management, and sent him to Tavistock. This was the beginning of the career in which he attained such eminence as a mining engineer.

In Cornwall he became acquainted with A. Woolfe, a self-taught engineer; they worked together with others in producing that splendid mechanical invention, the Cornish pumping engine. It is much to be regretted that Mr. Taylor did not continue the publication of his ' Records of Mining.' Only one volume appeared (1829) ; had it been continued, we should have had accounts of the progress of mining in Cornwall, and of his own labours. Though no mention of Woolfe and Taylor is found in English mechanical and industrial dictionaries, in the French. 'Annales des Mines' Mr. Taylor is named as a high authority, and he was held in much esteem by MM. Elie de Beaumont, Dufresnoy, and by the celebrated Baron von Humboldt.

Mr. Woolfe was the inventor of high-pressure steam worked expansively.

The first tunnel executed in England for the Tavistock canal through Morwel Down in 1806 was made under the direction of Mr. Taylor.

He wrote little; a few articles in the 'Philosophical Magazine' are all that I can mention.

In 1805 John Taylor married a sister of Captain Daniel Pring, R.N., whose family resided at Ivedon Pen, near Honiton. This proved a most happy union for himself, and a source of happiness to the whole Taylor family. My uncles and kinsmen held strong opinions, but were not very tolerant of others doing the same; the serene temper and supreme goodness of Mrs. Taylor softened all asperities, and for long years she was the peacemaker, the gentle adviser of her numerous relations.

In 1812 John Taylor quitted Cornwall and joined his brother Philip in establishing large chemical works at Stratford near Bow, London. Both brothers were good practical chemists, and they contributed to raise the character of that branch of manufactures, then in a very rude state., The firm subsequently added mechanical engineering to their other pursuits, but as competent judges considered John Taylor the best metallurgist in the country, and as he was strongly attached to his first profession, mining, he left his brother and devoted himself exclusively to that.

The 'Consolidated Mines' near Redruth, and many others in Cornwall and Devonshire, were placed under his direction; in 1820 and following years he undertook the management of the vast mineral property of the Duke of Devonshire, of Earl Grosvenor in North Wales, and of Greenwich Hospital in Cumberland.

In 1824 his frequent friendly intercourse with Baron von Humboldt led him to form a sanguine opinion of the mineral wealth to be found in Mexico. A company was formed for the purpose of working the mines of Real del Monte, the property of the Conde de Regla. Immense expectations were raised; the shares ran up to an unjustifiable height in spite of the warnings of Mr. Taylor.

Here I must mention a fine trait in John Taylor's

character.   He was often urged by kind friends to
make use of his special knowledge so as to profit by
the fluctuations of the market, and to realise a
fortune; these friends even offered to act for him,
that his name might not appear.   'I am an agent,
not a speculator,' was his invariable answer.   Pity
that his unostentatious rectitude has so few followers!

To return to Mexico.   The Board of Directors
soon found the difficulty of working mines in a
foreign, a distant, an uncivilised country.   Agents,
engineers, Cornish captains had to be sent out ; no
control could be exercised over them, and they soon
got to loggerheads.   The roads were scarcely
practicable, the Mexican officials did their part
in promoting disorder, and finally the English
company gave up the undertaking, which subsequently, in the hands of other parties managing it
on the spot, had great success.   I well remember
as a boy seeing the engines, pumps, and boilers at
my father's works, all made in detached pieces, not
one of which was to exceed a mule's load.   All these
had to be abandoned after the costly journey ; but
orders from head-quarters were months on their
way in those days, before steam and electricity had
conquered distance, and very great losses must have
been the result.

This untoward termination was a sore grief to Mr. Taylor; his efforts, however, were not unappreciated by the shareholders, as they made him a present of the valuable collection of minerals brought together by Dr. Babington at a cost of six hundred guineas, and home business had meanwhile been successful.

In 1823 an odd adventure befell my uncle. He was going down to Exeter by the mail coach, bowling along merrily at ten miles an hour, when at midnight a tremendous roar was heard, and some huge creature sprang on the leaders of the team; this proved to be nothing less than a royal Bengal tiger escaped from a wild beast show. The red-coated guard unslung his blunderbuss, not quite sure how to use it, when the keepers made their appearance, and with nets and tackle secured the ferocious but valuable animal. I was at my uncle's house when he came home and thrilled us by his description of the scene.

This same year Mr. Taylor was erecting some splendid water wheels for the Mold mines in Flintshire, of which he was manager; and he took a delightful house, Coed Dû, in the neighbourhood. Many foreigners and many Englishmen of the bygone generation long remembered the genial and

unaffected hospitality of Mr. and Mrs. Taylor.
Here is a letter from one of their guests, whose
striking features and charming manner I well
remember :—

35 Bury Street, St. James's.

'My dear Sir,—At my departure from Coed Dû
I was not able fully to express to you and to Mrs.
Taylor my gratitude for all the kindness you were
pleased to show me during the happy time I passed
in your house, and I thought to bury in silence
those feelings for which I could find but insufficient
expression.   However, being returned to this town,
and recapitulating in my memory every hour I en-
joyed since my absence from London, the recollec-
tion of your house and family must again and again
occur to my mind, and prevails upon me to address
you once more on this subject, though I am aware
of how little moment my thanks may be to you.
For you are accustomed to see everybody around
you happy, and indebted to you for their happiness
—the peasants, whose barren ground you have
changed into a fruitful garden, as well as your
happy children ; and accordingly you do not want
to hear repeated by a stranger the same feelings
which *they* may better and more properly express to
you.   But I myself cannot forbear uttering what

so strongly and most heartily I feel: restrained since long within the rules of ceremony, deprived of a familiarity to which I was accustomed before this journey, in short, after having been a stranger amongst strangers, I was received in your house like a friend. Absent for the first time from home and from my family, I had at least the pleasure of witnessing a happiness which at a former period of my life I shared myself. Those are the enjoyments which I owe to your and Mrs. Taylor's kindness, and I never shall forget them.

'If I should be so happy as to meet in my native land with you and your sons, or with any of your friends, I sincerely hope to find an opportunity of proving how much I feel indebted to you.

'Believe me, my dear sir,

'Yours very truly,

'FELIX MENDELSSOHN BARTHOLDY.'

Always anxious to help his fellow-workers, my uncle was actively employed in 1829 in the promotion of a mining school in Cornwall; this institution, the Polytechnic Society, I am glad to say, still continues. In 1825 Mr. Taylor had been elected a member of the Royal Society; he was one of the

earliest members of the Geological Society, and its
treasurer, 1816-44.

The first council of the British Association for
the Promotion of Science was held at his house
in Bedford Row in 1832.   Babbage, Brunel,
Davis Gilbert, Forbes, Vigors, Dr. Buckland, the
Rev. William Vernon Harcourt were among those
present, and Mr. Taylor was at once chosen treasurer, a post he occupied till 1860, when advancing
years compelled him to retire from his honourable
labours.   His descendants cherish the noble testi-
monial then given him by the council of the British
Association.

A full-length portrait of Mr. Taylor was painted
by Sir Thomas Lawrence, and presented to him by
seventy friends, shareholders in his various under-
takings; this picture was unfortunately destroyed
by fire in his son's house.

He was an active promoter of the London
University, and for many years its treasurer.

His love of mechanical inventions never abated.
He took great interest in Jordan's wood-carving machinery; but though that invention was charming,
witness the splendid carvings in the House of Lords,
the financial results were such that the company
had to be wound up.   Mr. Trollope recently told me

he had the plant in his workshops in Pimlico. My uncle was himself a very skilful worker in wood; he always had a supply of beautiful tools, and his dexterity with the turning lathe was very remarkable.

In 1863, at the age of 83, his honourable and useful life ended. I have attempted to sketch his public career, and to note his high moral standard.

He was succeeded in his business by his two sons John and Richard, both now dead. The firm is still carried on, under the old-established name of John Taylor & Sons, by the grandchildren of its founder.

Of Mr. Taylor's daughters, Anne, the eldest, married Philip Worsley, an active partner in Whitbread's brewery; his philanthropy and rectitude are well known. Their eldest son is a large chemical manufacturer near Bristol; another son has taken his father's place in Whitbread's brewery, and one daughter married a Roscoe, a member of the family which is known both in the world of letters and of science.

Susan, the second daughter, married Edward Rigby, M.D., a highly successful physician in London, and brother of the accomplished Lady Eastlake.

Honora, the third daughter, became the wife o
Edward Enfield, for many years an officer of the
Royal Mint.

These five children of my uncle John, the play-
mates of my boyhood, are all gone. I, the wayworn
hermit of the Mas d'Azil, remain behind, finding
some pleasure in retracing their lives, at the risk even
of being called garrulous. I hold, too—is it a mere
hobby?—that records of the beginnings of middle-
class families from which our bankers, traders,
manufacturers, engineers have sprung, our men of
letters and of arts, must be of interest not only to
their descendants, but to the future historian, who
desires to relate how the 'arts of peace' grew, and
by what individual efforts that growth was stimu-
lated.

The second son of Mr. John Taylor, Richard, was
born in 1781. He settled in London as a printer,
and was the friend and patron of Koenig, of printing-
press fame. Richard was a man of literary and
scientific attainments, and he was largely employed
in printing works in the dead languages and on
scientific subjects, and as editor of the 'Philosophical Magazine' he became known to most of the
scientific men in Europe. He was a Liberal—
almost a Radical—in politics; he had a love of

being in opposition; he was, however, a very useful member of the City of London Common Council for many years, and was held in high esteem.

He was a fine portly gentleman, and was thus alluded to in 'Punch':—

> When Corporal Taylor stalks the street
> A walking corporation.

He had some difficulty in sitting through the tedious civic banquet and still more tedious speeches, but at last he acquired the art of taking a nap during the most trying periods. This habit he carried into private life, and I well remember, at a dinner party at one of my aunts', her saying, 'Richard, will you take tart or pudding?' and then a tremendous rap on the table, and a stentorian voice saying 'Chair, chair! order, order,' as he woke up from his slumber.

He lived to be threescore and ten.

Edward, the third son, born in 1784, was a remarkably fine-looking man, with a deep bass voice and an ardent love of music; he was deeply versed in the history of music, and as Gresham Professor he achieved great success. An unflinching Liberal, an advocate of Parliamentary reform, he attended meetings in Norfolk and Suffolk to uphold his views, speaking well and boldly. The Government of the day had their eye on him. Once at a public meeting he pointed to a man, and said : 'That is a spy sent down by Lords Sidmouth and Castlereagh; he is welcome to tell them all I say.' He was spoken of in Parliament as 'a dangerous man,' but n the House of Lords Lord Albemarle, in the Commons Mr. Coke and Mr. William Smith, stood forth as his defenders, asking for proof of the assertions made, and declaring their intimacy with him. Some time later the informer Fayerman quarrelled with his employers, and published a letter, with a complete account of the transaction. My uncle was constantly holding intercourse with the leading Whigs, Sir Francis Burdett, Whitbread, Cobbett, and others. He dined with the Earl of Albemarle, meeting H.R.H. the Duke of Sussex, the Duke of Norfolk, Sir F. Burdett, Mr. Coke, &c. He dined with the Duke of Sussex in London, and on one occasion being seated in front of a blazing fire fainted away. The Tory papers got hold of the incident and attributed it to the Duke's wine.

In 1824 Mr. Taylor took a prominent part in promoting and organising the Norwich festivals. For the first festival he made the entire selection, he engaged all the performers, he chose the band,

and trained the choral society. Every oratorio brought out at these festivals till 1847 was translated and prepared by him. Among the number will be found Spohr's 'Last Judgment,' 'The Crucifixion,' 'The Fall of Babylon,' Mozart's 'Redemption,' Schneider's 'Deluge,' and many others.

My uncle made the acquaintance of Spohr on the occasion of a visit to Mendelssohn and his family at Düsseldorf, and became his intimate friend. He held him in high esteem, and placed him in the foremost rank of great musicians. When I looked at his stolid German countenance and burly frame, I felt some difficulty in believing him to be a great composer, but my uncle placed Spohr in the first rank of great musical writers. It was in 1830 that Taylor persuaded his friend to write 'The Fall of Babylon.'

Besides the Norwich festivals, my uncle was present at those held at Oxford, Salisbury, Derby, Liverpool, and York.

He joined his brother Philip in London in 1827 in the engineering factory in the City Road; but not relinquishing his musical pursuits, was elected Gresham Professor of Music in 1837, and held that post till 1863, when he died at Brentwood on the 12th of March.

Mr. E. Taylor married, in 1808, Miss Deborah Newson, of Norwich. By her he was the father of three children : John Edward, Kate, Margaret. John Edward had a highly cultivated mind and strong literary tastes. He died comparatively young, leaving a family of four children. His wife, Meta Dochow, has published translations from the German. Their son, Fairfax Taylor, is one of the clerks in the House of Lords ; he, too, writes well on various subjects.

Lucy, the eldest daughter, married Mr. Markby, a judge of the High Court at Calcutta for twelve years, and now holding a distinguished position at Oxford. Kate married Alfred Currey, grandson of Mr. Benjamin Currey, Clerk of the Parliaments in 1848, but for one day only, as he died shortly after his appointment.

The fourth son of Mr. Taylor of Norwich was my father, Philip, born in 1786. His life and career, with which mine is so mingled, I shall narrate later, and I therefore pass on to the fifth son, Arthur, also born at Norwich in 1790. In his early life he was in partnership with his brother Richard, but they soon separated. Arthur set up on his own account, and became printer to the City of London. His favourite study was archæo-

logy. He was a member of the Society of Anti-
quaries, and among the results of his studies was
the publication of ' The Glory of Regality.' He
married, in 1824, Miss Emily Lane.

The following anecdote illustrates the ardour of
his taste and temper. On his way to Italy he paid
a visit to my parents at Marseilles. On his way he
strayed into Autun, the ancient Augustodunum,
founded by the Phœnicians, seat of the Druids,
capital of the Ædui—what a field of exploration for
an antiquarian! so no sooner arrived at Marseilles
than with no word of explanation he disappeared
for three weeks, to our great anxiety. However,
back he came from this trip one morning, and
finding my father going out to look at a field just
purchased, Arthur went with him. Workmen were
turning the ground, to prepare for irrigation pipes,
when they came on some broken bits of tiles. My
uncle pounced on these, scraped them, tasted them,
declared them to be of the Roman period, and
placed them in safety to await further investigation.
He begged my father to have further excavations
made, and then continued his journey to Italy.
Meanwhile my father ascertained from an old
peasant that the spot was formerly a brick-field, and
as the irrigation works went on, this became more

certain, and the hoard of tiles was dismissed to the
rubbish-heap. But the first visit of my uncle on
his return was to the 'Roman tiles.' He asked my
father in sharp tones what had become of these
precious relics; and before the answer had ex-
plained why they were thrown away, he burst out
with 'You're a Goth, sir,' walked back to the
house, packed his portmanteau, and leaving a note
to say he would send for it, went to Marseilles, and
started for England, whilst we were waiting breakfast for him. It required long letters of apology,
and the gentle influence of mother, with whom he
was a great favourite, to calm down this irascible
'Monkbarns.'

Besides five sons, Mr. John Taylor had two
daughters. The eldest, Susan, born in 1788, was
married in 1807 to Henry Reeve, Esq. M.D. His
death at the early age of thirty-four was thus
alluded to by Dr. Sayers in the 'Norwich Mercury':
'Besides his acquirements in classical and other
literature, Dr. Reeve became well versed in the
primary object of his pursuit, and was no mean
proficient in the collateral studies of chemistry and
natural history.' His duties in private life were no
less happily discharged than those of his profession;
his mind was open, generous, lively, simple, and

affectionate; and those to whom he was united, as a relation or a friend, will ever turn with melancholy complacence to the remembrance of his faithful and active attachment, of his cheering conversation, and of his valuable accomplishments.

Two children of the marriage, Susan and Wallace, died in their infancy. Henry, born in 1813, was henceforth the sole object of his widowed mother's care. She went to reside at Geneva for his education; there she found friends of her husband, and there her son came to know the De la Rives, the Candolles, Sismondis, De Roches, the families Lombard, Binet, Hentsch, Maunoir, Roget.

Mrs. Reeve was loved and valued by her Genevese friends as she deserved to be. Courage, good sense, refined tastes, and simple habits were her most marked characteristics. To her last hour she preserved undiminished the love for her husband so early taken from her, whilst proud of the career of his son. She died in 1864, aged 76.

Early in life Mr. Henry Reeve began his career as a man of letters. His natural gifts, aided by an education carried on at Geneva, Munich, and Paris, seemed to point in this direction. His first work was a translation of 'Democracy in America' from the French, and he became the close friend of its

authors, Alexis de Tocqueville and Gustave de
Beaumont. Then came translations of Guizot's
writings.

The Marquis of Lansdowne, whose acquaintance he made through his aunt, Mrs. Austin, was
struck by Henry Reeve, and gave him a place in the
office of the Privy Council, and for fifty years he
has held the office of Registrar of the Judicial Committee. On the retirement of Sir George Cornewall
Lewis, who was appointed Chancellor of the Exche-
quer in 1855, Mr. Reeve was appointed to the
editorship of the 'Edinburgh Review,' to which his
father had been, in 1802, one of the earliest contri-
butors.

Sarah, the youngest daughter and last child of
John Taylor, was born in 1793. She married John
Austin, the well-known writer on jurisprudence.

Sarah Austin was a well-known figure among
the cultivated women of the first half of this century.
She was endowed with great intellectual powers,
which her education had developed ; she had rare
social talents, great beauty, and astonishing industry.
Her first important work was a translation of Prince
Puckler Muskau's 'Book of Travels in England ;'
then came a translation of Ranke's 'History of the
Popes.' When the author received Mrs. Austin's

translation, he wrote to her that, after reading it, he felt obliged to retranslate his own work into German—a rare tribute of approbation, coming from such a man. She wrote various books on Germany, yet always found time to help her husband in his learned and abstruse labours. She was a frequent guest at Bowood and at Lansdowne House. She had many friends in Germany, whilst in her salon in Paris she received the leading men of the day —Guizot, Mignet, Barthélemy St.-Hilaire, the poet Auguste Barbier, Victor Cousin, Count and Countess de Circourt, the Say family, Madame de Peyronnet, Auguste Comte, and others.

Of Victor Cousin, the philosopher, I must relate an anecdote. We had been with my aunt to a *fête* at St.-Cloud, and on our way home M. Cousin undertook to sing a ballad describing a visit of a Parisian to this popular fair. With expressive gesture and hands clasped over his breast, he carolled forth—

Et mon cœur était pris aux filets de St.-Cloud.

Though a boy when I heard this, I still see his saturnine countenance, and hear his chuckles at the joke implied ; for the nets are also those of the police stretched across the Seine to catch the unfortunates who seek to commit suicide.

D

In each of her residences, London, Bonn, Dresden, and Paris, Mrs. Austin succeeded, though with very limited pecuniary means, in attracting the most cultivated society to her house.

She was honoured by the friendship of Helena, Duchess of Orleans, and the sons of that admirable princess, the Comte de Paris and the Duc de Chartres, inspired her with the deepest interest and regard.

In 1834 Mr. Cornewall Lewis and Mr. John Austin were sent as Royal Commissioners to examine into the state of Malta. Mrs. Austin accompanied her husband, and the trio passed a few days at my father's at Marseilles, waiting the arrival of the 'Vernon.' That ship, then the crack frigate of H.M. navy, had to work up against contrary winds, and when she arrived was in quarantine; so the captain requested the Royal Commissioners to embark without delay. All was in confusion at this sudden departure, and the washerwoman had not sent back the linen. Mr. Austin, who rarely smiled, and issued his mandates in stern and brief sentences, stood in the hall, and in a stentorian voice thundered forth: 'What does the woman mean? Go and *wrest* the things from her.' Well I remember the scene.

I cannot tell what were the labours of the two clever commissioners, but I know that thirty years after, when I had to transact some complicated insurance business with the agent in Malta, I casually asked the lawyer if he recollected my uncle Mr. John Austin. 'What!' he replied, 'are you the nephew of Mrs. Sarah Austin, whose name is so honoured and revered in Malta, and who has left such marks of her presence amongst us? You her nephew, and not at once say so!'

My business was transacted with the greatest facility, and I passed some pleasant days with the old friends of my aunt.

Curiously enough, I renewed acquaintance with H.M.S. 'Vernon' the other day (1884) at Portsmouth, when I was the guest of my old friend Captain Drury of the 'Excellent.' The 'Vernon' is now the torpedo school ship, and was commanded by another old friend, Captain Markham, of Arctic renown.

Mr. Austin suffered from attacks of hypochondriasis, which interfered with his completing his writings on law and jurisprudence. His lectures were, however, very remarkable, and he was much occupied with the reform of legal procedure. At Mr. Austin's death, his papers, including the preparatory notes, were in sad confusion; his widow undertook the task of arranging and putting them into shape for publication, and, as the 'Times' said in a review of the work, never did wife raise a nobler monument to the memory of her husband—it may be added, nor show her own remarkable literary power.

Mr. Austin's brother Charles was the celebrated parliamentary counsel.

John Austin died in 1865, and my aunt in 1867 at the age of 73. Their only child, Lucy, beautiful and accomplished, was well known in society as the wife of Sir Alexander Duff Gordon, Bart. She too translated and wrote. 'The Amber Witch,' 'Letters from the Cape,' and 'Letters from Egypt' are favourite books with all who have read them. Failing health took her to Africa, and among strange races and stranger ways she showed her sympathetic nature, learning their language, studying their manners, helping them in their troubles. Poor Prévost-Paradol speaks of her conduct when a pestilence broke out on the banks of the Nile: ill as she was herself, she stood forth among the terror-stricken population as doctor, nurse, consoler, and her noble self-sacrifice was repaid by the devotion of the Arab tribes.

Lady Duff Gordon died at Thebes in 1869,

Sir Alexander in 1872. He was succeeded by their son Maurice, born 1849. Janet, the eldest daughter, married Henry Ross 1860, and lives in Italy, where, like her mother, she loves to study and describe the habits and dialects of the peasantry. Urania, the youngest child, who was brought up by her great-aunt, Miss Charlotte Austin, died in her sixteenth year.

I now revert to the children of Richard and Margaret Taylor (born Meadows). The fourth son, Meadows, lived at Diss, and succeeded his uncle, Philip Meadows, as a solicitor. His grandson, Francis Taylor, was elected in 1885 to represent the Diss division of the county of Norfolk in the House of Commons.

The fifth son, Samuel, lived at New Buckenham, in Norfolk, and devoted himself to agriculture. His neighbours looked up to him as a practical farmer, and his journals of farming operations are quoted with high praise in the 'British Farmer's Magazine.' It is interesting to note some of his facts. In 1779 the Norfolk labourer received a shilling a day and a pint of beer. In 1770 it was usual to sow six pecks of wheat per acre; now on Lord Leicester's and Lord Western's land at least three bushels are sown or drilled. In the disastrous year 1800 wheat fetched 6l. 10s. per quarter; in 1803 an abundant harvest sent down the price to 2*l.* 14*s.* ; in 1818 the tod (28 lbs.) of wool sold for 4*l.* 4*s.*, that is, 3*s.* a pound.

Mr. Samuel Taylor lost his wife in 1795. Though only thirty-four, she was the mother of seven children ; and his sisters Margaret and Sarah henceforth took charge of their education and the management of his household. Small of stature, but full of energy, were those prim ladies, with their precise ideas and modes of life, and rigid views on the education of children. Well do I remember their enforcing them on my juvenile mind when I was staying at Buckenham, perched up in my small chair at table. I was given a piece of plum-cake ; I pulled out the plums, and made a little heap, to be able to eat them all together as a *bonne bouche*, and was going on with the dough, when a voice was heard to say, ' Children must not be greedy,' and invading my platter with her spoon, my aunt conveyed the plums to her own mouth. *I* may have been wrong, but was *she* right ?

Samuel Taylor's eldest son—also a Samuel, and a farmer - took great interest in local politics, wrote squibs and songs, and was active at elections, of course on the Whig side. He became manager of Whitbread's malting establishment, near Thetford.

TAYLOR FAMILY OF NORWICH.

Mr. S. Taylor married Miss Newson, but of this marriage there was no issue.

The third son, Richard Cowling Taylor, born in 1789, was brought up to be a land surveyor. He was a first-rate geologist, and constantly associated with Mr. William Smith, the father of English geology. But before railroad enterprise existed, there was little employment for a man like him; and just before Stephenson's genius opened up a career for civil engineers, R. C. Taylor accepted a mining post in the United States. Pity he should have quitted England, for, besides his professional acquirements, he was no mean antiquarian. His ' Index Monasticus of the Diocese of Norwich and the Kingdom of East Anglia ' is a work of great research, and was thus acknowledged by Sir Walter Scott:—

Edinburgh, 16th April, 1821.

' Without such a work the study of history is a labyrinth without a clue; while, on the contrary, the guidance which your work affords facilitates at once the acquisition of truth and the detection of error. I remain, with a deep sense of obligation,

' Sir,

' Your very obedient servant,

' WALTER SCOTT.'

In 1848, Mr. R. C. Taylor, then living at
Philadelphia, published his important work on the
statistics of coal.   He collected and classified all
the information from all parts of the world on this
subject, reducing the various weights and measures
to English standards.   To proprietors of mines and
collieries this work is essential for reference and information, whilst to the general reader it is full of
interest as giving an account of what forms the
basis of the industrial prosperity of each country.
He was a member of various learned societies in
Europe and America.   His death took place
whilst carrying out some surveying operations near
Chagres.

Mr. R. C. Taylor married, in 1820, Miss
Errington, of Great Yarmouth.   There were four
daughters of this marriage.

Thomas, the fourth son of Samuel Taylor, was
a sufferer from poor health, and sought the climate
of the south of France and then of Pisa, where he
died in 1838.

Edgar, the fifth son, was a lawyer.   I quote
from the 'Legal Observer,' 1839, the following
eulogium :—

'To his professional talents it is not easy to do
justice.   He was a man of a very acute mind, and

remarkable for his foresight and generalship. His own personal practice was principally in the equity courts. In the early stages of the most complicated suit he delighted to look forward and to provide for contingencies which could not occur till the cause had advanced to stages requiring years to arrive at. His memory was such that, on the contingency taking place, he had the whole previous arrangement in his mind. Though latterly the suits under his charge were very numerous, yet he always bore the particulars of each in his mind : the object of the suit, the parties to it, and the state in which it was. He rarely had to give two readings to any cause, however long its duration. Altogether, a man better fitted to the management of the most extensive business, even in its minutest details, can scarcely be conceived.'

To this notice of his professional talents I must add my tribute to his generous nature and his true friendship. When my father was attacked by a company ready to sacrifice an honest man to their greed, Edgar came to his help, unravelled the web they sought to spin round their victim, and finally triumphed over his assailants, and showed my dear father's character to be unblemished.

Mr. Edgar Taylor's professional labours, heavy

as they were, did not preclude his indulging his
strong literary tastes. In 1838 he published 'The
Book of Rights,' a digest of constitutional law from
Magna Charta downwards. He was an accomplished.
antiquarian and a fine Greek scholar ; in his will
he leaves to his widow his manuscript translation
of Griesbach's edition of the New Testament. He
was a great lover of German literature. Children
delighted in his 'German Popular Tales,' older
readers in his 'German Minnesingers,' his translation of Master Wace's Chronicles of the Norman
Conquest, from the 'Roman de Rou.' His anony-
mous contributions to periodical literature, legal,
theological, literary, were very numerous. I here
break off to give another letter from Sir Walter
Scott.

'I have to return my best thanks for the very
acceptable present your goodness has made me in
your interesting volume of German tales and tra-
ditions. I have often wished to see such a work
undertaken by a gentleman of taste sufficient to
adapt the simplicity of the German narrative to our
own, which you have done so successfully.'

I have heard my father say that Lord Brougham,
then Chancellor, tried to induce Edgar Taylor to
enter public life. Several reasons were given for his

refusal; that he gave my father was, he did not wish to be tied to the tail of a comet.

Edgar Taylor married in 1823 Anne, daughter of S. Christie, Esq., a wealthy merchant. It was said that, after the engagement was declared, Mr. Christie sustained great losses from speculations in indigo, and friends of Mr. E. Taylor suggested he should throw over the lady; Edgar's answer was, 'I marry the lady, not her fortune.'

Mr. Edgar Taylor's health, always infirm, gave serious cause for anxiety in 1832, and in 1839 he died. His industry was never checked, whatever his bodily sufferings might be. His memory is held in honour by all who knew him. His widow survived him, and there was one daughter.

A sister, Jane, married Mr. John Martineau, later on a partner of my father. Another sister, Emily, was herself an authoress and a poet. Her 'England and its People,' for children, a volume of poems selected with great taste, as well as some of her own composition, are well known, and in her correspondence with my mother I find proofs of her reading, her taste, and her judgment of literary subjects. Emily Taylor died in 1873.

PART II.

My father, Philip Taylor, the fourth son of John and Susannah Taylor of Norwich, was born in 1786, and received his earliest training under the eye of· his excellent mother. He was, after due consideration, educated for the medical profession, and at fifteen he was sent down to live with his brother John at Tavistock, and to study surgery and medicine under Dr. Harness, a relation of Mrs. John Taylor. From London, where he stopped on his way to Cornwall, he writes to his mother that he had breakfasted with Mr. Denman, had been to the theatre, but disapproved of the play, which was one of Lewis's, and that Mrs. Jordan had not a proper part assigned to her. I do not understand why my father was not articled to one of his kinsmen, distinguished surgeons in Norwich; his medical education under Dr. Harness was very desultory, and he took more interest in the mineral and engineering works of Taylor and Wolffe than in Dr. Harness's surgery, and after a few years returned to Norwich. There he joined Mr. Fitch in a large business as chemist and druggist, and set

up a factory for making wooden pill-boxes by
machinery; and in 1812, in concert with his brother,
he started chemical works at Stratford in Essex.
Some capitalists were associated with the Taylor
brothers : 1 infer from letters now in my possession
that the Ricardos were among them.

A fine field seemed opened to practical chemists,
for the manufacture of ' chemicals ' was in a very
rudimentary state.   John Taylor gave his attention
chiefly to metallurgical chemistry, Philip to the
mechanical side, notably to the reorganisation of
apparatus. The inventive spirit of these young
men was sometimes held in check by their moneyed
partners, as may be inferred from a note at the
foot of an elaborate notice on the manufacture of
oil of vitriol (now called sulphuric acid) in 1815 :—

1846.—These experiments were made by me immediately after Davy had published his theory of the
formation of sulphuric acid. My reasoning on the
subject was better than the apparatus at my command,
and yet my apparatus was better than the partners I
had then to deal with; they not encouraging me, I let
the things drop, and many years after others reaped the
profit and the credit of the process herein suggested.

These checks did not, however, arrest the inventive efforts of the brothers; in 1816 and 1818 my

father took out his patent for the application of high-pressure steam to the purpose of evaporation; and about the same time, in concert with his brother, he launched the idea and project of using oil for the production of gas. These inventions were independent of the chemical factory.

In 1813 my father married Sarah, only daughter of Robert Fitch, a surgeon at Ipswich. The Fytche family in the sixteenth century were owners of Little Canfield Hall. At the coronation of George II. William Fytche, lord of the manor of Fingreth, Essex, claimed the office of Chamberlain to the Queen on the coronation day, with H.M.'s bed and furniture as a fee, but this claim was not allowed. My grandmother's name was Borett. Her brother had a mechanical genius, and was the inventor of that apparatus which has become a necessity in the houses of all civilised countries. It is recorded in the family that Borett was Artificer to the Royal Palaces, and that George III. was very fond of watching him adjust the valves and traps. One night at the play, the king was in his royal box, Borett in the pit, when a man sitting next to him started to his feet and levelled a pistol at the monarch's head. Borett, seeing the movement, struck up the madman's arm, and the ball went through the ceil-

ing. A great uproar ensued; then His Majesty
came forward, bowed to the excited audience, and
in a loud voice said, ' Thank you, Borett; thank ye,
thank ye.' In France a decoration and a coat of
arms would have been given Borett, with heraldic
pistols, pistons and pans, ' armes parlantes,' as the
phrase goes.

In the year 1815 my father settled at Bromley
near Bow, and soon after I was born, a sister being
the first child.

Three events marked the four years of my
infancy : the first misadventure was near akin to
sacrilege ; the second well-nigh sent me to an early
grave ; the third was a charge of murder and the
loss of a fortune. Number one was at my christen-
ing, which took place in our drawing-room on
account of my mother's health being delicate.
After the service there was to be ' a tea.' The
servant brought in an urn with boiling water, but
the pastor, who was seated near my mother, and
who was very near-sighted, jumped up, said, ' Ah !
here comes the dear child again,' and threw his
arms round the scalding urn—a loud howl was the
result. The second was my being taken out driving
by my cousins ; they were discussing what road they
should take, but not minding that on which they

were driving—result, an upset, and little Phil being
pitched on his head on the sharp angle of a broken
stone step.   It was touch and go with little Phil,
and who knows whether the 'arraignée dans son
plafond' does not date from that day?

My third adventure was indeed tragical.   There
dwelt in Abingdon Street an old aunt of my mother,
the widow of an Indian colonel.   Mrs. Robertson
had ample means, was very fond of her niece, and
very kind to her little 'great-nephew.'   I often
was taken to the house and allowed to sit up at the
dinner-table.   Mrs. Robertson's hall was adorned
with Indian trophies; there were tigers' heads with
real eyes, there were skins of all manner of ferocious
beasts; but among these dead creatures, slain by
the defunct Colonel, there was one living creature,
the favourite of his mistress.   Now either Poll was
jealous of me, or he had a special love of my small
white legs; for one day as I toddled upstairs cling-
ing to my mother, and trembling at the big game,
Poll, without one warning croak, sprang at my
uncovered calf.   Frantic with pain and fright, I
clutched his neck, and over we rolled to the foot of
the stairs.   I was picked up and taken to the kitchen,
where my tears were dried, my hands washed, and
many caresses were lavished.   No caresses could

bring Poll to life, but as the noise had not reached the dining-room I took my seat as if nothing had occurred. Now my great-aunt's butler 'Smart' was a surly fellow, not approving small boys and their ways. On this particular day Smart's shoes creaked, his mistress complained, he growled out he 'couldn't help new shoes creaking,' and there was a tiff, then a silence, and Mrs. Robertson asked to have 'her pretty Poll' brought in. No answer. Then she turned to Smart. 'Where is Poll?' 'Ask young master,' the fellow cried, with a hideous grin, and the murder was out. The old lady looked aghast for a moment, then collecting her ideas she said, 'Call a coach.' The coach came, she pointed to the door, and in solemn tones gave sentence: 'Madam, I allow no murderers in my house.' My frightened mother hauled me away, and she left, never to re-enter the house. Mrs. Robertson declined all overtures, and, dying, left her large fortune to some people named Garlic: they did not come forward to claim it, and the Crown stepped in.

I return to my father's schemes for gas made from oils. In 1739, Clayton first drew attention to the fact that gas for lighting purposes was to be obtained from coal; in 1792, Murdoch, who was Watt's right-hand man, made great advance in

E

the practical application, and lit up his house at
Redruth with gas. The Cornish miners told a
story that Murdoch, who was in the habit of
carrying a bladder of gas as his lantern, was
waylaid one dark night, on his way to his lonely
house, by highwaymen. He gave the bladder a
squeeze, sent a jet of flame on their faces, which
singed their whiskers, and then exploded, and
before they could recover from the fright Murdoch
had made good his escape. He had a curious gift
of estimating work, and would say to Mr. Watt,
'Now, sir, you please to see what it comes to with
your figures; I'll just step down and chalk it out on
a bit of board.' When the results were compared a
discrepancy would appear. 'Ah!' said Murdoch,
'you have figured too fine, sir, you have not taken
into account casualties.'

I must pause here to observe that eighty years
ago the mechanical engineer had none of the
splendid self-acting machines or tools which now
exist. Whitworth, Maudslay, Fox, Nasmyth, had
not yet arisen; the hammer, the chisel, the file, were
the only implements; the very lathes were in their
infancy, the slide rest was hardly thought of; yet
from these rude beginnings sprang the splendid
science of mechanical engineering. I will now

quote from Mr. Frederic Accum's work on coal-gas, of which he was a strong partisan, the following report (published 1819) :—

Messrs. J. and P. Taylor are the first persons who have resorted to oil as a substance from which gas for illumination can be easily and cheaply prepared. The apparatus for the purpose is much smaller, much simpler, and yet equally effectual with the best coal-gas apparatus. The retort is a bent cast-iron tube, which is heated red by a small convenient furnace, and into which oil is allowed to drop by a very ingenious apparatus ; the oil is immediately volatilised, and the vapour in traversing the tube becomes perfectly decomposed ; a mixture of inflammable gases which contains a great proportion of olefiant gas passes off ; it is washed by being passed through a vessel of water (which dissolves a little sebacic acid, and which seldom requires changing), and is then conducted into the gasometer. The facility and cleanliness with which gas is prepared from oil in the above manner may be conceived from the description of the process. A small furnace is lighted, and a sufficient quantity of the commonest oil is put into a small iron vessel; a cock is turned, and the gas, after passing through water in the washing vessel, goes into the gasholder. The operation may be stopped by shutting off the oil, or to a certain extent hastened by letting it move freely on ; the small quantity of charcoal deposited in the retort is drawn out by a small rake, and the water in the washer is very rarely changed.

This new process attracted public notice, and my father visited many towns to plan and erect the necessary apparatus. Covent Garden Theatre and several large factories and breweries were lit by this gas.

The Emperor of Russia ordered the Taylor apparatus to be used in the Imperial Library at St. Petersburg, and for a few years its triumph seemed secure.

Meanwhile, the coal-gas makers saw their danger, and set to work to improve the process of manufacture and the system of purifying. They sold their gas for fifteen shillings the thousand cubic feet, the oil-gas was charged fifty shillings the thousand cubic feet, whereas only thirty-four shillings should have been the price, and it should have been made clear to the public that five hundred cubic feet of oil-gas gave as much light as a thousand feet of coal-gas. Five years after the discovery, in 1823, the battle of the gases took place; but the combat was unequal, large companies had been formed, large sums subscribed to manufacture coal-gas; applications were made to the House of Commons for charters, committees of investigation were formed, the Taylors had to stand alone against the combination of the wealthy promoters of these companies, and the engineers and managers to whom they held out hope of employment, and they were beaten.

The evidence given on behalf of coal-gas was hardly honest, but my father accepted the decision and gave up his plans, consoled to a certain extent by the sympathy of such men as Brand, Charles MacIntosh, Ricardo, Clément Desormes, the French chemist, and others.

Now I revert to the patents for the application of high-pressure steam for evaporating processes, taken out in 1818. It became desirable to construct the apparatus on their own premises, and for this purpose the brothers acquired some buildings in White Cross Street formerly occupied by Koenig. My father had a high opinion of his printing-press inventions, and vindicated poor Koenig's claims in a paper contributed to the 'Philosophical Magazine' in October 1847. John Taylor's real interest was mining engineering, and, as I have stated in the sketch of his life, he separated from my father in 1820.

Up to this period the only known application of steam to boiling or evaporating purposes was by applying the vapour to the external surfaces of the vessel containing the liquid; this led to an enormous

waste of caloric. Philip Taylor introduced the steam
in coils of pipes into the body of the liquid. Messrs.
Whitbread at once adopted this plan for their
brewery; sugar refiners at home, sugar planters
in the West Indies, beetroot sugar growers in
France, applied for the apparatus, recognising its
great superiority to the old processes.

The soap-works of Messrs. B. Hawes were the
scene of a difficulty and a triumph. The curd
completely stopped the passage of the heat by
coagulating round the steam coil. My father was
awake one night turning the matter over; next
morning he sought the soap-makers, told them the
mode of dealing with the problem, and, with a
promise of secrecy on their part, allowed them to
purchase his invention—a very simple one when
put in practice—a small pipe with minute perforations to allow the escape of steam was introduced
when the soap-curd became too consistent, a jet of
high-pressure steam was injected by the means of
these perforations, and the coil was cleared. That
Messrs. Hawes thought the secret well worth keeping
I had an opportunity for judging in 1833. I called
at the works; the reception was courteous, but I was
not allowed to see the boilers. Mr. Hawes, however,
asked me to breakfast with him next day, a pleasure

which was not to be mine, as it turned out. On Saturday evening I went to Mr. Babbage's conversazione, where, after watching him grind his calculating machine and explain its functions to two old maids, I was carried off to speak French with Lady Morgan, by whose side I took my place, having Lady King (Lord Byron's daughter) on my left. Mr. Hawes sauntered past us, and as soon as it was decorous to move, I followed him ; then Michael Faraday seized me to ask news of his old friend, my father. On my return home (that is, to uncle John's), I found a note from Mr. Hawes expressing his regret at not being able to receive me, as he had to leave town suddenly.

A year before uncle John retired a new partner joined the firm, John, son of John Martineau, one of the partners in Whitbread's Brewery. My father writes of this arrangement: ' I can truly say I engage in my new partnership with every desire to be happy, and to contribute to the happiness and prosperity of my comrades, but I may be excused if I have doubts and fears.' Partners and patents rarely brought luck to my father.

The premises in White Cross Street were not large enough for the constantly increasing business, and the large factory in the City Road was opened.

Bromley House became a centre of attraction for men of science of all nations; it was lit with oil-gas, the laboratory was admirably equipped, and steam power was at hand for experiments and demonstrations. There were gardens and paddocks, whilst access to London was made easy by a stage-coach twice a day. True, there was an Irish colony in the lanes near, turbulent neighbours, but the venerable priest who had charge of them was a French *émigré* of noble birth, and from him I learned the rudiments of the language I have spoken for sixty years; and I see now his silver locks as he sat with my mother and heard her read French, which she too was destined to use in her daily intercourse for many a long year.

I see, too, the hatchet face of MacAdam, the road maker; the cheery countenance of Captain MacArthur, who first introduced sheep into Australia (Botany Bay in those days); and pleasant Charles MacIntosh, my father's chemical crony; Michael Faraday, always modest and retiring, whose Cornish blood was recognised as well as his genius; Dr. Wollaston, who cut jokes at my father's expense, 'a man who pretends to persuade gas to walk through pipes;' Brunel of block-making fame, the future tunneller, then struggling with the Admiralty;

Professor Clément Desormes, one of the most eminent practical chemists France has produced; Biot the biologist; Gay Lussac; Mallet of the Ponts et Chaussées, afterwards Chief Inspector, who was so fond of England—he always began his lectures with ' Nos voisins d'outremer ;' Paul Séguin, who made the first railway in France (Lyon et St.-Etienne), Baron von Humboldt, and many German professors.

Then there were chance visitors who came to ask technical advice. On one occasion my father and a few friends were making experiments with protoxide of azote, otherwise laughing gas, and a bladder full with a quid attached was just got ready when one of these visitors, a future Chief Baron, came in. He was so interested in the explanation of its properties that he insisted on trying in person what were its effects. He took a pull àt the bladder, imbibed a tremendous dose, dropped on all-fours and careered round the laboratory table. My mother and I were in the garden, and, hearing a hubbub, went to see what had happened. My father and his friends were frantically pursuing the lawyer, who was still running round and round on all-fours, barking like a dog. At last the bladder was wrenched from his mouth, but hours elapsed before the effects of the dangerous dose ceased.

Many a tale of those days and those men linger
in my memory. Here is one of Maudslay. In his
youth he was a private in an infantry regiment.
His colonel had scientific tastes and scientific
instruments; one of these was given by the nurse
to little master, who dashed it out of the window,
and it fell in pieces before the colonel's eyes, to his
unutterable dismay. The stalwart sentry looked at
the bits, and, saluting, said, ' Weel, colonel, I think I
could set it to rights.' ' You ? ' ' Oh yes, colonel, if
you will let me try.' The colonel ordered the
sentry to be relieved, entrusted him with the broken
instrument, and rewarded his skill by obtaining the
soldier's discharge and starting him on that path of
life in which he obtained such eminence.

I must not omit an anecdote of Rennie. He, like
Michael Faraday, was a blacksmith in his youth.
When a successful engineer he was invited by a great
Scotch noble to visit him at his Highland castle.
Mr. Rennie set forth from Edinburgh in a post-
chaise, and was struggling along over the bad roads
of those pre-MacAdamite days, when he perceived
a carriage which had broken down ; he courteously
invited the two travellers (they also were bound for
the castle) to share his chaise, and on they went. A
rougher road and a deeper rut caused such a jolt that

one of the tires broke. Luckily a Highland blacksmith was at hand. 'I could mend it, but I have no
one to strike to me.' 'Is that all?' said Rennie.
'Come on;' and in a minute he had taken off his
coat, tucked up his shirt-sleeves, and with a 'Now,
my man, set on,' was at work. The fastidious young
dandies looked with disgust at their fellow-traveller
blowing the bellows and then lifting the ponderous
hammer and dealing well-directed blows on the red-
hot metal. ''Gad, man, but ye know ye'r trade,'
quoth the Highland smith. The work was done, on
went the chaise, but no longer did the dandies
converse affably; indeed, their demeanour became
hardly civil. At length the chaise drew up at the
castle, and out rushed the Duke with both hands ex-
tended, 'Ah, Mr. Rennie, how glad I am to see you!'
The young swells shook their curly heads, and
uttered that society and the constitution were
going to the dogs.

There are stories, too, of French friends. My
mother had sitting on each side at her dinner-table
a great French chemist, when one of her sneezing fits
set in; up rose each gallant Gaul with his hand on
his heart: 'Dieu vous bénisse, madame!' and then
a profound bow, further sneezing, 'à vos souhaits,
madame,' and deeper bows, and so on, whilst my

father stared at his over-courteous guests, and I, seated on his knee, made free use of the glass of port just poured out. Then burly Clément Desormes would show his friendly feelings by taking my father in his arms and kissing him on both cheeks. It was Desormes who, with Brunel, and J. B. Say, the French ambassador, a frequent visitor to the City Road works, urged my father to visit France, holding out hopes that the Government might adopt oil-gas for public buildings. So in April 1822 my parents made their first visit to Paris, where Desormes, Bréguet, Arago, Firmin Didot, J. B. Say, and their wives did everything to make their stay a pleasant one. My mother spoke French, my father at the end of fifty years in the country had not mastered the language. ' Je n'ai jamais connu personne qui eût eu le don de massacrer le français du Roi comme votre bon père,' said Admiral Charles Baudin to me one day.

Whilst my father was in Paris he received some letters from Marc Brunel, which I shall now give. They show the friendship as well as the business relations which existed between the two men.

Chelsea : April 19, 1822.

My dear Friend,—You have, I have no doubt, found plenty of employment besides your business in the great capital ; if the weather has been fine, you must see everything in the first order, and in the most striking colour, for nothing can be so delightful as the first green of spring, which in Paris must be the more beautiful as the atmosphere is free from that foggy tinge which spoils everything here, and even at Bromley or Chelsea.

I have not troubled you with anything of my own, because it is well to be silent until something is done here. The French are not so very enterprising in these matters as we are here, therefore if a thing is not taken up at once it is likely to retrograde rather than advance. I shall be glad to know how *you* have succeeded. In case you wish to introduce your printing-press there, the best channel I think is that of M. Firmin Didot. He was here the week before last, he called on me with the view of seeing my stereotype, but I would not gratify him, nor was it likely to be interesting to him, for whatever may be the ultimate degree of perfection it may reach, it is now limited to one object only.

My son Isambard, who, I am told, is much grown, wrote me he had seen you ; I hope you will bring me a good account of him.

The coal-trough has not yet come to Chelsea ; it may reach it to-day, however. I am impatient to see it put up. I am busy preparing two bridges for the French Government. All is going pretty well. The press is getting on. Best regards to Mrs. Taylor.

Yours very truly,

Mᶜ. I. BRUNEL.

April 26, 1822.

My dear Sir,—I have received your letter about
M. Lainé, who was already provided with leave to see
the dockyards, with good recommendations from the
Admiral and the Commissioners at Portsmouth, where
he is gone by this time.

I am very much pleased with the account you give
me of your intercourse with the scientific men ; I don't
know how far you are master of the French language,
without which you must lose a great deal of the enter-
tainment which such society must afford.   Our worthy
M. Bréguet is a man whom one must regret not to be
able to exchange sentiments with.

I do hope Mrs. Taylor is able to enter into the diver-
sions which the capital abounds with.   The eyes may
find extensive range though the ears may prove but
helpless interpreters.

My son regretted as much as you may have done in
not being of the party at M. Bréguet's when you dined
there.   I learn through my son that gas, such as it is
established in Paris, is not only very bad, but is ex-
tremely offensive.   I do hope they will have sense
enough to be convinced of what I have strenuously recommended, which is oil-gas.   It was my opinion, and
that opinion was conveyed by the late French ambassador, but some folks only looked to the *job*, without
minding the consequence under the specious mark of
economy.

By the bye, M. Lainé had a letter from his uncle, the
late Minister, to me, with whom I have had much to do in

relation to the waterworks. He expresses his regret
that the negotiation should not have been brought to a
favourable issue. I found him well disposed to have
countenanced the enterprise, and if he was still in power
you might have found an able administrator in him,
and with liberal views.

The coal-trough is just up, but the rack and pinions
I had ordered from Maudslay are not yet come. Patience
is necessary in all schemes. If you can sell some of the
machines in Paris they had better be sent. The directions could be translated there. I imagine Isambard
will do it well. How do you find him? I so long to
have him back. Best regards to Mrs. Taylor.

Yours very sincerely,
Mᶜ. BRUNEL.

P.S.—What do they do in the steam-engine line?
Would it answer to bring anything forward in that way?
If you have any copying presses with you I hope they
won't omit the directions and the dampers.

In a memoir of the life of Sir M. I. Brunel, published in 1862, my father made a note, expressing
his surprise at finding no mention of their joint
labours or their friendly relations. He hints that
it might have been remembered that in the catastrophe of 1821 he was one of the first to come to
his friend's aid. He states that in 1822 he to
out a patent of an improved press (referred to by
Mr. Brunel in the above letters), and finally he

writes, 'Not only has my name been omitted in connection with my old friend, but at page 209 of the book the writer gives my brother John's name instead of mine at the first general meeting of the Thames Tunnel. That I was director, and I may add the most active one, up to 1825, the following document shows :—

Thames Tunnel Office, Walbrook Buildings.

Extract from the minutes and resolutions of the Court of Directors, held April 26, 1825.

'No. 10. A letter having been read from Philip Taylor, Esq., expressing a wish to resign his appointment of director in this company, on account of his numerous professional engagements and his expected residence chiefly at a distance from London :

'No. 11. Resolved that Mr. Taylor's resignation be accepted, and that the clerk do write him a letter expressive of the regret which the court feels in being deprived of his valuable services as director of this company during the progress of the works of the tunnel.'

(Extracted by Chas. Butler, clerk to the Company.)

I believe there still survive two watermen (in sugar) who took part in the banquet given on the occasion of laying the first stone of the tunnel by W. Smith, Esq., M.P.; a complete model in sugar of the tunnel decorated the table, and my father brought home the two figures.

In 1830 I visited Mr. M. Brunel at the Thames Tunnel, and his kind reception of me dwells in my memory. It was soon after one of the great eruptions of water, I was taken to the workings, and when I reached the shield, and some of the old hands found out that I was my father's son, they hoisted me up into one of the cells, and I had the honour of doing a bit of excavation.

Isambard Brunel was at school with Alfred Say (son of J. B. Say, and uncle of my wife) at the Institution Massin, Place de l'Estrapade, Paris. After the custom of French schools the boys were taken for a walk on Thursdays; they passed a long deep tub set out to water the cab-horses, when a mischievous schoolfellow jerked up the horse's nose; he threw up his heels, hit Isambard on the seat of honour, and sent him head foremost in the dirty water, from which his comrades dragged him half choked, after wasting a minute or two in laughing at the catastrophe.

Before leaving Mr. M. Brunel, I wish to note the constant aid and friendship shown him by Sir Samuel Bentham during those vexatious disputes with the Admiralty when he was employed in erecting his block-making machinery. Sir Samuel was one of my father's correspondents, and I give

F

an extract from one of his letters showing his active mind on various subjects : —

Montpellier : Sept. 19, 1822.

I understand that grafted are to be preferred to ungrafted mulberry trees. My mulberry trees succeed exceedingly well, not having suffered from the great drought of the year ; so that I shall, if possible, plant another thousand of large trees in a state not to suffer by the sheep, and perhaps twenty thousand young ones in places from which the sheep will be excluded. It will be two years at least before we shall have leaves enough to feed a sufficiency of silkworms for it to be worth while to engage any one for the management of them, and then we must erect a building for that purpose. The squash or vegetable marrow which we have cultivated these two years, besides being good food for ourselves and others, we find so very prolific that we propose cultivating them in great quantity next year for pigs. The two boars we brought have arrived safe. Notwithstanding the general prediction of their failure, they are in good health, but as yet rather too young to be of any use. All our men, as well as our money, have been so extensively employed in planting and breaking up new ground for cultivation, besides the necessary repairs and additions to buildings, that we have not as yet been able to erect the pumping machinery from England ; we hope, however, to begin it in about a month, and I am determined to provide means of working the pump by wind, in such a manner as to work night and day without attendance.

Then comes a long disquisition on self-regulating windmills, a request for my father's opinion, and a promise to send the ounce of Chinese silkworm eggs, already announced. I can only guess that my father was to make experiments with the leaves of a large old red mulberry tree growing in the Bromley garden, and said to have been planted by James I. to supply silk for the Royal hose—a mistake to plant the red sort, it should have been the white mulberry.

Sir S. Bentham's ounce of seed ought to have given 42,000 worms, and they would require 400 or 500 square feet of space, and in the fifth period about three tons of leaves per diem.

I return to my parents' stay at Paris, where my mother listened to the silvery tones of Mademoiselle Mars and the splendid declamation of Talma. My father's business, however, made no progress; here again coal-gas had enlisted the support of important men, and when it was suggested that some opposition might be overcome by the present of an Indian shawl to a ballet-dancer, my father's Puritan principles were roused, he took his wife by the arm, and left Paris and the Parisians to their darkness, their dirt, and their evil ways. But one incident which befell my father I must not leave out. One

F 2

day in the Tuileries Gardens he spied a vacant chair and sat down. Now when a French lady takes her ease she requires two chairs ; one to sit on, the other as a rampart and a footstool. My father had not observed that two dainty feet rested on the chair he had appropriated, and he could not understand the loud tones and fierce gestures of 'le mari de madame.' Fortunately John Bull was not in one of his irascible moods, still he kept possession of his seat. 'Monsieur' produced his card, and mischief might have ensued, but for the intervention of an officer who understood English and soothed the wounded feelings of his countryman. After a few minutes' conversation it turned out the young officer was a near relation of General de Bardelin, who when an *émigré* at Norwich had given French lessons to my aunt.

My parents travelled home by the Rhine and Holland. No *Dampfshiff* existed in those days, a boat had to be hired, and, moving slowly on by day, travellers slept on shore. One evening the hostelry my parents stopped at had a sinister look, and in the middle of the night my mother was awakened by a noise at the window ; she looked and saw a man trying to open the casement. Without disturbing her sleeping husband, my mother got out of

bed, seized a log of wood from the hearth, and
hurled it at the German invader; down he went, and
with him went the window.

My father's efforts to interest the Dutch in oil-
gas had been no more successful than at Paris; they
sailed to Harwich, and thence came to Ipswich,
where I was staying with my grandfather Fitch. Of
course the first thing my parents were asked was if
they had eaten frogs.

I now pass on to my father and his friend
Charles MacIntosh's experiments in the preparation
of waterproof textures, the difficulty being to find a
cheap solvent of the india-rubber. Mr. MacIntosh
had for years been occupied with the subject. I
will give extracts from his letters:—

Cragsbasket July 21, 1822.

Our friend Mr. R. has informed me of your return to
England. During your Continental tour you must have
amassed much valuable as well as much amusing matter,
and I am convinced you could favour the world with
sketches of a very different and infinitely more amusing
kind than any that have yet appeared; perhaps you
have something of the kind in view, a comparative view
of the arts, &c., as at present in actual practice in France
and Britain. I hope this is the case.

I have not yet proceeded in taking out the patent for
my coal-oil caoutchouc varnish—not from any doubt as

to its importance, or the many valuable purposes it is applicable for, but because patents form a sort of property I confess I am by no means partial to, having often reflected with disgust on the great trouble and vexation as well as loss of time and expenses our bleaching liquid (oxymuriate of lime) patent cost me, which I justly considered an original and valuable invention, yet the patent was set aside. Now I could not lay claim to the discovery of caoutchouc being soluble in coal-oil, because it is on record to be so, and possibly it may be concluded to follow from inference, at least, that it must have been tried as a varnish before I did so : although if such is the case, the success must have been very trifling, else the thing would have been persevered in, and we should have heard of it.

I can with all confidence assure you that coal-oil, when properly rectified, dissolves caoutchouc vastly more rapidly than ether does, employing about two pounds of caoutchouc cut in shreds to four gallons of coal-oil, by which means, and employing frequent agitation, it is soon brought into a pulpy gelatinous state, to be afterwards diluted to any degree of consistency required. It then forms an admirable elastic varnish for cloth of all sorts, as well as for metals, &c., which dries almost immediately, leaving the caoutchouc altogether unchanged, possessing all its original properties. For umbrella cloths alone it will prove of great importance.

In a box I despatch this day will be found addressed to you two quart bottles, one filled with naphthalic varnish, the other with coal-oil for diluting the former to the proper state for use. I shall certainly feel very greatly obliged by your making at once some trials, and reporting as early as possible your opinion of them. I need hardly add to you that rectified coal-oil dissolves common resin, camphor, and many other resinous bodies with the greatest facility. I pray you to write me soon, and with my best regards to Mrs. Taylor, in which Mrs. MacIntosh most cordially joins,

I remain, truly and faithfully yours,

CHARLES MACINTOSH.

This letter gives not only an account of the progress of an invention which has been of universal benefit, it shows Mr. MacIntosh's opinion of patent rights; later on a patent was well-nigh his ruin. About 1830 Messrs. Neilson and MacIntosh dis-covered that great improvement in the manufacture of iron, the application of the hot blast—my father joining them; and on the same day and hour patents were taken out in London by Neilson and MacIntosh, in Paris by Philip Taylor. This in-vention brought large fortunes to the ironmasters, whilst to the patentees it brought years of toil and anxiety, and two formidable lawsuits; I shall speak of that in the French courts later on. I have lived with and among inventors, have watched them work out their ideas with painful labour and self-sacrifice; at last the moment of triumph is at

hand, fame and competence in view; they draw up
their specifications and apply for a patent, pay the
fees, and receive the precious document. Meanwhile
their specifications are being overhauled by dishonest
rivals, who either treat the invention as futile or
seize on it for themselves. Then begin struggles in
law courts with judges and juries to whom chemistry
and engineering are mysteries. Not every suitor
could command the services of such a counsel as
Edward Sugden, who, when he had to defend a
patent for a great chemical invention, went to a
laboratory, worked out each process himself, was
a complete master of the subject, and making a
speech which was a splendid lecture on chemistry,
won his cause. But too often the inventor's work
is filched, and the jury, who could understand if your
purse were stolen, are utterly unable to understand
'infringement of patent.'

I will give another extract from Mr. MacIntosh's
correspondence with my father :—

Feb. 20, 1824.

Dear Sir,—I saw your cousin, Mr. Fitch, the other
day when I called at your works, and had some conversation with him about preparing the waterproof varnish
for me to be produced from the tar spirit we may contract
for from the London Chartered Gas Company, and which
may probably be only 800 gallons a week. . . . It would

be very gratifying to me if you would examine and rectify the samples I send you ; . . . possibly you may devise means of diminishing the smell, which would be a great desideratum. . . .

CHARLES MacINTOSH.

It was whilst my father was intent on these experiments that he met with an accident which was nearly fatal. The real name of the rectified coal-oil was naphtha, one of the most volatile and inflammable substances known. Late one night, having rectified the oil, he was going on with his experiment, and, in so doing, he decanted the liquid into a Florence flask which he very imprudently had laid on a warm sand bath. The naphtha was instantly volatilised. An unfortunate gas-burner was alight near ; the inflammable vapour ignited, the flask exploded, and every particle of hair and skin on my poor father's head was destroyed—that his eyes did not suffer was a miracle ; he was a dreadful sufferer for some days. His friend MacIntosh was full of sympathy, and he ought to have been consoled by thinking of the millions who would be kept dry and warm by his discovery.

Professor Clément Desormes sent a specimen of petroleum about this time to my father, with the suggestion that it might be of use for making oil-gas,

but the supply was, he went on to say, limited—
things have changed now that Russia and the
United States can furnish any quantity of petroleum.

The years 1823 and 1824 were a very busy time
for Philip Taylor. First comes his application of
high-pressure steam to sugar-filtering—this was
largely used by foreign sugar-refiners and beet-sugar-
makers. French writers give it high praise for its
compact yet enormous filtering surface; English
writers seem silent on the subject. The other filter
used in France is that by Dumont, a very clever
construction; it is used alternately with the filter
' Taylor '; often have I heard the foreman issue the
order, ' Charge the Taylor,' ' Empty the Dumont.'

About this time my father made his experiments,
and published his tables on the elastic force of
steam. Mr. Dalton had compiled his table from
32 degrees of temperature to 212 degrees, and from
0·200 force in inches of mercury to 30 inches.
Philip Taylor started from Mr. Dalton's finishing
point, and carried the experiments from 212 degrees
to 320 degrees, and from 30 inches of mercury to
179·40.

MM. Arago and Dulong repeated these experiments, and I had the pleasure of hearing from M.
Arago, that only a slight difference existed between

their results and my father's; their experiments were carried higher than my father's, but the three tables are published in France in juxtaposition. It is somewhat strange that Fairbairn, in his 'Useful Information for Engineers' published in 1856, does not notice Philip Taylor's tables, though he does those of Dalton, Arago, Dulong, Regnault, and De Pambour.

The apparatus used by my father was a clever combination: the boiler was heated by oil-gas jets, the lofty manometer went through the floor of our nursery, as well as I remember. The quantity of gas consumed was noted down with the other results.

A new subject of study was the water supply of London. My father proposed starting from a point between Brentford and Richmond, constructing a tunnel or waterway of six feet diameter and about nine miles length, to the foot of Hampstead Hill; from thence the water was to be raised by a perpendicular lift to the reservoirs, and the splendid working of the Cornish pumping engines would have been brought into play. By this project the great loss occasioned by forcing water through a long range of pipes would have been avoided; it was calculated that a saving of three-fourths of the coal used in the working of the steam engines would be effected.

The estimates for the tunnel, the engines, and
the reservoirs, were put down at 180,000*l.* For this
sum London might have had good and cheap water;
but the scheme fell through—I know not why.

A Swiss engineer, M. Bodmer, a man of inventive if not practical genius, came to England and
claimed my father's good offices to extricate from
the clutches of the Custom House authorities the
drawings and instruments he had brought from
Zürich and Aarau, then famed for these things.
Through the help of Sir Samuel Bentham, M. Bodmer got back his property. He settled at Manchester,
and was very intimate with my father. Another
engineer with whom my father corresponded was
Fawcett of Liverpool. He wished my father to join
his house; perhaps it is to be regretted that he
refused. Subsequently my brother Robert was a
pupil and a favourite of Mr. Fawcett. It may be
remembered that the engines of the ' President,' lost
in 1841, were built by Fawcett.

Well, besides experiments in the realm of science
there were experiments in education, and I was sent
to a school at Bromley kept by Mr. Deane. Even now
I see the long room, in each corner a high desk, at
these desks masters for separate subjects, Latin and
French, &c. ; at the end a throne, where was installed

the pedagogue himself. Each morning at eight o'clock
he opened the doors of a big stand which was part
of his throne, and displayed an assortment of canes ;
then he blew his nose, and in a stentorian voice read
the reports of the masters, the names of the culprits,
and proceeded to inflict punishment ; the more
numerous the culprits, the better pleased he seemed,
retiring to his breakfast rather sadly if the canes
had not been used. There were whippings at home
also. My father always rode to and from London,
and entered the house with his riding-whip under
his arm. ' Oh, my love,' said my dear mother,
' Phil has been so naughty ; ' then I found myself
athwart my father's knee, down came the whip, and,
howling, away I went to the nursery to meditate
some future misdemeanour.

Dear old father ! when he had passed eighty and
I was near sixty we had a talk over those days.

Father. ' Yes, you were an unruly child ! what
trouble you did give ! '

Son. ' No doubt, sir, but you should not have
used that riding-whip so lavishly on my hide.'

Father. ' You don't mean to say, you—you recollect that ? '

Son. ' Don't I ! Why, those lashes for years
rankled in my mind ; I believe each stripe made me

worse than before. It is my misfortune to appear
to forget, but always to recollect.'

Father. 'Well, you are a perverse sample of
human nature. Now, you can't say that you did
not merit punishment.'

Son. 'Not always.'

Father. ' Now, *now*, for instance, I recollect when
you behaved so ill about that glass of rhubarb and
magnesia. You were sick, stomach out of order,
and I prepared a nice little dose to set you right.
What did you do? Why, sir, you upset it. I mixed
another. What did you do, you young imp? You
threw it at me, all over my shirt front and waist-
coat. Did you deserve no whipping then?'

I am unable to discover when, or with whom, my
father went to Newcastle to see and report on the
first locomotive of George Stephenson, though his
description of the first attempts is still vividly
before my mind.

My father's examination before a committee of
the House of Commons is to be found in the Blue-
book.   .

In 1823 he took out the patent for his horizontal
steam engine. He had dared to take the steam
cylinder out of its vertical position, and put it in a
horizontal position, and was for this assailed by the

jokes and gibes of his brother engineers. Brunel suggested various difficulties, customers declined new-fangled notions. Maudslay, however, in 1824 or 1825, erected an engine for pumping water out of the Thames Tunnel, of which the cylinders were at an angle of 45° (the pumps were made by Taylor and Martineau). My father's specifications being for horizontal cylinders, the patent was easily infringed by keeping a little clear of the horizontal. The wording should have been ' for all cylinders not vertical ; ' as it was, though Taylor and Martineau made a considerable number of these machines, my father received no direct benefit from his invention.

In the year 1824 we left Bromley House for Abercarn House (in South Wales), the property of Sir Benjamin Hall, afterwards Lord Llanover. The house stood in a lonely valley ; opposite were the wooded cliffs of Craig Darren ; the gardens sloped down to the rushing waters of the Ebbw. There was a village green, one quaint old public-house, a chapel in which a Welsh parson preached in his native tongue, and I had a Welsh pony called 'Ross,' on which I scampered about, and was occasionally greeted as a young dog of a Sassenach by the sur- rounding Celts. We were joined here by young Alfred Say, son of the Professor of Political Economy,

Jean Baptiste Say, and destined to be my uncle
by marriage. We had very kind neighbours in Mr.
and Mrs. Hanbury Leigh, of Pontypool Park. But
our stay was not to be long in this peaceful spot ; my
father had come there in connection with the works
of the British Iron Company, and he had to move to
Corngreaves for the same reasons. I forbear to enter
into any particulars of this company, and its disastrous influence on my father's affairs ; enough to
say his character was vindicated by Lord Lynd-
hurst's decision in 1832.

In 1827 my father discovered that his own
business, which he had left thriving, had got into
difficulties, and it required all his courage to look
matters in the face. Amongst other incidents Mr.
John Martineau, his partner, had listened to a
German chemist who professed to convert pig-iron
at once into steel ; yet the scheme, which then was
a failure, was an anticipation of that which in
Bessemer's hands became a splendid success.

A few months before the catastrophe, Marc
Séguin, the well-known French engineer who made
the first railway in France (that from Lyons to
St. Etienne), came over to England to consult my
father on the form of the rail to be adopted. In
the correspondence which ensued on the fish-belly

rail, Séguin writes of 'your parallel rail,' and I possess a wooden model of a parallel rail which my father always kept, though I am unable to verify his claim to be the originator of this form, now in universal use.

M. Séguin learned through this correspondence the position in which my father found himself, and he wrote asking him to come at once to France to organise a large iron factory to be erected near Lyons. At the same time my father's staunch friends, Clément Desormes and J. B. Say, urged him to come to Paris; the Duke Decazes, Louis XVIII.'s minister, wanted to start iron works in his department, the Aveyron, whilst M. Berard wished to form a company for the same purpose at Alais near Nismes. By the desire of Clément Desormes a complete model of the Abersychan works had been made and sent to the museum of the Conservatoire des Arts et Métiers. This model established my father's reputation as an iron-maker in France.

Whilst friends in France pressed him to come among them, one of my father's truest friends at home, Edgar Taylor, advised him to leave the care of his defence in his hands, and in 1828 my parents withdrew from the strain and anxieties which beset them, and began life again in France.

On my father's arrival in Paris he looked into the various offers made him by companies, and decided not to accept any of them. He found good and remunerative occupation in importing English machinery. He fitted up several large sugar refineries and beet-sugar factories, amongst others that belonging to the son and grandsons of Santerre the Sansculotte. The first ball I ever went to was given by M. Santerre at his splendid mansion in the Marais, once belonging to a great French noble.

He had much to do at Chatillon, formerly the property of Marshal Marmont, Duke of Ragusa, then the marriage portion given to his daughter by Ouvrard, the army contractor and speculator. He put up a large beet-sugar manufactory there, and many others for people without historical names.

In 1831 my father took his old pupil and young friend Alfred Say into partnership, and another person, who proved so unsatisfactory that the firm was dissolved.

In 1829, Neilson and Charles MacIntosh's invention of the hot blast for iron-making caused a revolution in Great Britain, and I may say the world. Mr. Philip Taylor was interested in the French patent, which was taken out in his name, whilst that in England was in the name of MacIntosh;

this was in 1830. The French iron-makers were slow in recognising the value of this invention.

A short time after the Revolution of July 1830, Mr. MacIntosh asked Philip Taylor to take as a partner a young Frenchman whose career as an officer in the Guards had come to an end by the exile of his king. He had, I believe, married a connection of Mr. MacIntosh. Whilst Mr. Taylor was engaged in plans and arrangements for the apparatus, the young partner, active, intelligent, and agreeable, though not always discreet, travelled all over France to rouse the attention of the ironmasters. The new process gained ground, and as the patentees took a royalty on every ton of iron made, the invention became lucrative. Some of the smaller ironmasters, however, could not see the justice of paying for 'warming their wind,' and a squabble between the French partner and a customer coming to reinforce the discontent, an attack on the hot-blast patent was set on foot. The French patent law declared that if an invention had been made public in print in a foreign land, a patent could not be obtained, or at least be valid in France. The paragraph which followed escaped the observation of the enemy, who sent agents to Scotland in search of printed matter. After a minute search at Glasgow, they found an obscure working men's paper which contained a short notice of an improved process for making iron, due to Mr. Neilson. It was stated that he used warm air for the blast. Back to France came the agents with this precious document, and legal proceedings were at once begun.

The cause came before the Tribunal of First Instance at Paris in April 1836.   The judge, aware that the suit would go into appeal, and unwilling to go into scientific evidence, declared the patent void and unduly obtained.   The cause was then heard by the Court of Appeal in Paris in the following month of August; again Taylor et Cie. were beaten, the patent was declared *abusive*, and the decision of the lower tribunal was upheld; but the 'juge rapporteur,' in framing the decree, put in a phrase of his own, stating that the court found the invention of too great national importance to be left in the hands of an individual, and that individual a foreigner. The patentees now submitted their case to the High Court of Cassation.   That supreme French court of justice quashed the previous judgments, first because the Court of Appeal had no mission to decide on the merits of an invention, but merely to decide if the law on patents had been complied with; and secondly, because the proof proffered in the shape of the

Glasgow paper was not sufficient, the law in one of its clauses stating that the mention of an invention must be worded so as to enable any one to be able to put it into use. The simple enunciation of a new theory was not sufficient, details as to the application must follow; and the Court of Cassation sent the case to be tried before the Court of Appeal of Amiens. On May 18, 1839, that court gave judgment in favour of Taylor et Cie.

But by this time the patent was within a few months of expiring, whilst the long years of litigation had enabled ironmasters to use the process free of royalty, only a few high-minded men sending in statements and paying what was due; even those sums in the management of the young guardsman seem to have been lost.

I must not omit to state that in 1834 my father received the large gold medal for his apparatus, which was in the great exhibition of that year.

At the request of MM. Arago and J. B. Say, Philip Taylor prepared a scheme for the supply of water to Paris; few cities stood in greater need, as those who remember the Auvergnat water-carriers in the streets and staircases of Paris will admit.

The project was to bring the waters of the Marne, a tributary of the Seine, by a tunnel under the centre of the hill of Ivry, which stands on the left bank of the Seine high above the city, then to sink shafts, and raise it to the top of the hill by means of Cornish pumping-engines. This plan was simple and easy of execution, and the Marne could furnish a large body of water, though, as the name implies, not quite clear. To remedy this, large filtering beds were to be formed on the crest of the hill. These projected filters were on a new system; they were to be low arches of rubble stone, covered over with layers of coarse gravel and fine sand: the water introduced underneath would have risen through the gravel like natural springs.

One remarkable point was the facility of cleansing the filters by reversing the operation. The complete plans, after much trouble spent in preparing them, were submitted to the Council of the city of Paris by the two members Arago and J. B. Say; but the Government corps of engineers had a voice in the matter, and they objected to the scheme of an outsider and a foreigner.

His Majesty Louis Philippe, having heard of the proposal, expressed a wish to see the plans, and my father was received at an audience in the palace of the Tuileries. In the course of conversation the King showed my father the price at which wine for

the royal navy was supplied, calculated the cost
of water to the poorer classes in Paris, and pointed
out that wine was cheaper than water. His Majesty
appeared to approve highly of Mr. Taylor's views,
and went on to converse on other topics—the difficulty of making the Palace comfortable, above all
of introducing modern sanitary arrangements (my
great-uncle Borett should have been present).

The King spoke of the lamented Mr. Huskisson
and the great esteem he felt for him, adding, ' When
he was last in Paris he came to see me at Neuilly,
and I asked him if he thought that the French
nation had improved. " Well, yes," replied Mr.
Huskisson, " yes. You don't wear such shocking
bad hats as you did." '

Altogether a gratifying interview with Royalty ;
but it was all the reward my father had for weeks
of labour and boxes full of drawings and plans.

Another topic of interest to Mr. Philip Taylor
was the projected Canal des Pyrénées, to unite
Bayonne with Toulouse and the Mediterranean ;
but the new railway system put canals out of
favour—a mistake, as in England, with much heavy
traffic, people are finding out.

In 1833 my mother's health gave some cause
for anxiety, a warmer climate than that of Paris

was recommended, and my parents determined to move southwards. For many years my father's attention had been directed to the future of the Mediterranean Sea as the promised waters of steam navigation, and towards, if not to, Marseilles he directed his steps. Of course timid persons tried to deter him ; but, as if to ensure decision, the owners of large corn-mills at Marseilles for whom he had erected two powerful steam-engines offered him the management of the concern and a share in the profits. In those days Marseilles had the privilege of grinding wheat in bond for exportation, and the offer made my father sounded very advantageous.   Shortly before accepting the offer, he had been in Italy studying both in Piedmont and Lombardy silk-spinning and winding (an industry to which his correspondence with Sir S. Bentham when he was at Bromley refers), and making friends with whom he could easily negotiate from Marseilles.

In 1833, therefore, my father joined MM. Marliani and Labbey at Marseilles, and for the first year the corn-mills ground merrily ; then the landed proprietors found out that grinding foreign wheat in bond and exporting the flour was the destruction of wheat-growing in France, and agitated against the mills. The deputies did not understand the question, but they did understand that their elections depended on destroying the bonding system. The Ministers tried to resist the pressure put on them, in vain; such stringent measures were carried that the manufacture of flour had to be abandoned, with the result that the United States took it up.

And so once again Mr. Philip Taylor experienced the vicissitudes caused by Government interference, and possibly the difficulty of partnership; but he was not discouraged, and reverting to his real vocation, mechanical engineering, he determined to test the question of making Marseilles the starting-place of steam navigation. His two eldest sons were now of an age to help him, a piece of land was purchased, and in the last month of the year 1836, Philip Taylor, with his sons Philip Meadows and Robert, laid the first stone of the works which became the important and extensive Compagnie des Forges et Chantiers de la Méditerranée. In 1845 the large shipbuilding establishment of La Seyne opposite Toulon was opened.

Five men sufficed for the business when first started, now it gave employment to more than two thousand, and the Government was so well aware of

the benefit to Marseilles and to France of my father's
efforts that in 1846 he was made a Knight of the
Legion of Honour.

It was in this year that my father, influenced by
the wishes of M. de Cavour and M. d'Azeglio, went
to Genoa, leaving the management of the works at
Marseilles to his sons, where he planned and erected
a splendid engineering establishment at San Pier
d'Arena. Then came the storms of 1848, the battle
of Novara was fought and lost, the Piedmontese
treasury was empty, and the subsidies promised by
the unfortunate King Carlo Alberto were not forth-
coming. I shall not now enter into the complications
and troubles, some of them political, which ensued ;
enough to say that in 1850 Mr. Philip Taylor
returned to his peaceful home at St. Marguerite
near Marseilles, receiving before he left Genoa, at
the hands of General La Marmora, the cross of
St. Maurice and St. Lazarus, which King Victor
Emmanuel conferred on him.

But now came a blow of quite a different kind,
and one under which my father's heart indeed sank.
In the short space of two years four of his much-
loved children were taken from him by sudden
deaths, three sons and one daughter. . . . My
brother Robert, his father's pride, my other self,

only so far above me, died at Pau, of consumption. Even now, when thirty years have elapsed, I cannot bear to dwell on the sorrow that his death caused.

The weight of responsibility was now all on my shoulders. With my father's consent I went to Paris; and, by the help of the Say family, a company was formed to take over the concern, and so ensure ease and comfort to my father.

Here I will break off, as my own life had become so mingled with that of my father and his undertaking that I must be more conspicuous, and give some account of the education and the training which was to fit me for my career.